Merry Christmas 2000
From Tim, Theresa + Girls

D1278180

Praise for Michael Podesta's *Alleluia: Words of Praise*

"We are so familiar with the words of Scripture—especially the most precious and beautiful ones—that in time they tend to lose their power for us. It is the great gift of Michael Podesta to help us hear and see them again, almost as if for the first time. This is both a book to treasure and a call to prayer."

Frederick Buechner
Author, *Peculiar Treasures*

"I have known Michael Podesta for the past twenty years, and I have been thrilled by so much of his artwork. Nearly everywhere I travel I see that others have similarly appreciated his unique calligraphy. Michael takes familiar words of Scripture and turns the words themselves into art. Their appeal crosses all denominational and cultural lines and the artwork becomes a focal point and conversation starter wherever it is displayed. It is a delight to see these forty-two designs combined into a single book, and Michael's commentary enriches their impact and meaning."

John W. Howe
Bishop, The Episcopal Church, Diocese of Central Florida

"What can I say about the visual and verbal feast that is *Alleluia?* The book speaks for itself. Indeed, it sings for itself. This is a book by a man who notices the thing most worth noticing: how the Redeemer God of glory intersects our world and our experience. No abstracted theory here. This is a book of both joys and sorrows, both repentance and obedience, both conversion and consummation. It is, most of all, a book of faith, arising from faith, inviting faith in our Lord Jesus Christ. I commend both the book and its author for commending such a One to us."

David Powlison
Editor, *The Journal of Biblical Counseling*

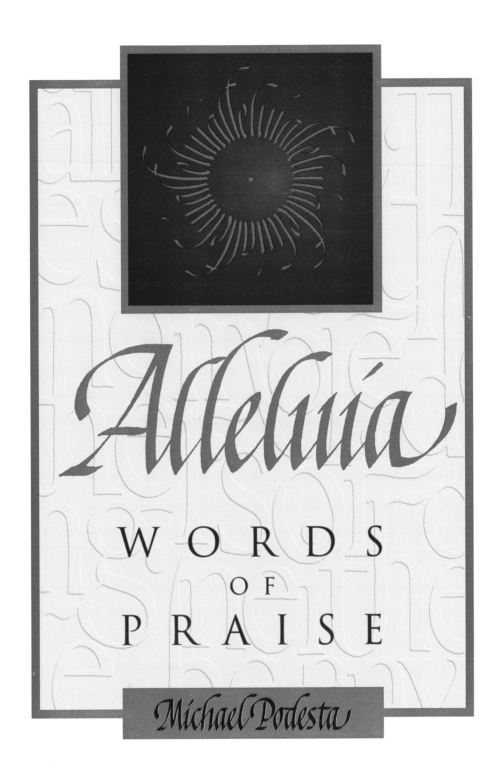

Alleluia

WORDS
OF
PRAISE

Michael Podesta

OLIVER
NELSON

THOMAS NELSON PUBLISHERS
Nashville • Atlanta • London • Vancouver

Published in Nashville, Tennessee, by Thomas Nelson, Inc., Publishers, and distributed in Canada by Word Communications, Ltd., Richmond, British Columbia.

Library of Congress Cataloging-in-Publication Data

Podesta, Michael.
  Alleluia : words of praise / Michael Podesta.
       p. cm.
    ISBN 0-7852-7339-5 (hardcover)
    1. Bible—Meditations. I. Title.
  BS483.5.P63   1997
  242-dc21   97-14153
                                                                        CIP

Printed in the United States of America.

2 3 4 5 6 — 02 01 00 99 98 97

For Kezziah

CONTENTS

PREFACE

I share these words of praise from the setting of my beliefs and activities. The symbolism in the artwork is personal, as well as general; the Scripture is often a paraphrase or a combination of translations.

Family, work, friendship, the seasons, music, memory. These are the experiences in which I have seen the line that separates the "spiritual" from the "secular" blur and then completely disappear. These are the experiences in which I have found God's good gifts and tender mercies sufficient to the needs of everyday life.

he Hebrew word *hallel* means "praise," and *Yah* or *Jah* is shorthand for "Jehovah," the Lord, so "Alleluia" is derived from "Praise the Lord."

In the book of Revelation, a heavenly multitude shouts, "Alleluia! For the Lord God Omnipotent reigns! Let us be glad and rejoice and give Him glory."

We use the word as an exclamation of praise, joy, thanks. Its overwhelming repetition in the choruses of Handel's *Messiah* is probably one of the reasons I not only hear it over and over, but see it that way, too.

ALLELUIA

t an art show, when people say, "Looks like most of this is from the Bible. How come?" I often answer with a parallel:

"I enjoy cooking. If you happen to drop in at our home, in trying to make you feel welcome, I would ask, 'Are you hungry?' If you say 'yes,' then your meal will be the best, the freshest, the most wholesome food I can find. These collected Scriptures also are sustenance, and they are the best I could find."

O taste, and see that the Lord is good. psalm 34:8

wanted the letters to be close, to touch and intertwine. Also, the oval format seems to accent the conjugal theme. On another level, the blending of blue into green suggests a merging of heaven and earth.

In my understanding, through the bridegroom and the bride, Solomon offers us a symbol of God and His people. But is there not yet another meaning to these words, one that relates to our own marriages? In Genesis, God said it is not good for us to be alone. His gift to me is my beloved. Holding and being held by my beloved are both gift and worship.

*S*hortly after our first son was born, my wife and I decided that he should have a birth announcement. I remember that the whole process of his entry into our lives—except for a few of the basic details—seemed to me essentially mysterious. Books on prenatal development, consultations with the obstetrician, and even contact with friends and their young children did nothing to dispel an abiding sense of awe. When these words from Psalm 139 came to mind, they gave me the idea for Alexander's birth announcement:

> I will praise thee; for I am fearfully and wonderfully made: marvellous are thy works; and that my soul knoweth right well. My substance was not hid from thee when I was made in secret, and curiously wrought in the lowest parts of the earth. Thine eyes did see my substance, yet being unperfect; and in thy book all my members were written, which in continuance were fashioned, when as yet there was none of them. How precious also are thy thoughts unto me, O God! How great is the sum of them! . . . And when I awake, I am still with thee.

ALEXANDER

*S*ome translations say, "Children are a gift of the LORD." When I consider my gifts, or blessings, and those of my friends, I feel certain that the greatest of these must be our children. This gift is, in its potential certainly, the most creative, the most godlike. This is the gift in which we share the love God shares with us, and so become, as parents and as families, participants in creation.

The mystery of the Spirit become flesh is wrapped in a blanket in my arms, and I am singing "Summertime" to help him get back to sleep.

CHILDREN

are a heritage of the Lord. psalm 127 verse 3

When I am talking to my children or other young people and we come to the subject of jobs, I try to share my view of the difference between a career and a vocation. You may choose a career, but a vocation chooses you.

When one is "called," that is a vocation. "Whom shall I send? Who will go for Me?" was a summons, a "calling" to Isaiah. It was crucial that Isaiah was listening; I hope that I am listening; I hope that my children are listening.

I have considered my use of *Me* instead of *Us* in "Who will go for Me?" and feel it is an expression of a personal, one-to-one relationship. "Will you [Michael] do this for Me?"

✛ ✛ ✛

I was lettering a wall menu for a friend who was getting ready to open a sandwich shop the following week. I had just finished a very handsome "Blueberry Muffin with Cream Cheese" when everyone—the plumbers, the electrician, the cabinetmaker—stopped for a morning break. Looking for something to read while I drank my coffee, I picked up someone's pocket Bible. "For I am persuaded," Paul said in his letter to the Romans, "that neither death nor life, nor angels nor principalities . . . nor any other created thing, shall be able to separate us from the love of God."

I finished my work on the menu, but something had changed. I wanted to use the alphabet to share words like Paul's.

The German graphic designer Rudolph Koch said, "The scribe is the servant of the text." My experience in the sandwich shop meant that a larger text beckoned to me.

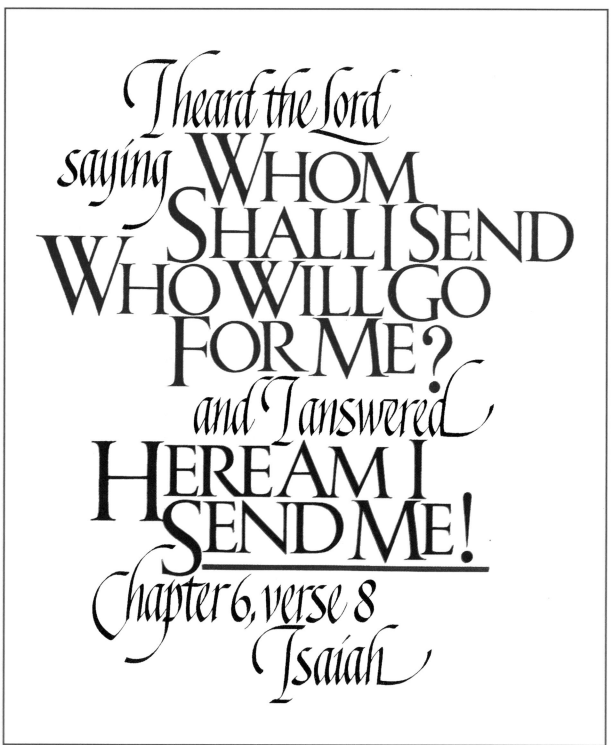

I heard the Lord saying WHOM SHALL I SEND WHO WILL GO FOR ME? and I answered HERE AM I SEND ME!

chapter 6, verse 8 Isaiah

*T*hese words tell us to be quiet, calm, attentive. There is a time to listen—as Isaiah listened. Our lives move so fast that sometimes it seems the only way we can participate is through ever-increasing productivity and speed. So we get very involved; we embrace activity; we busy ourselves. We talk on the phone—or perhaps via the computer—much of the day and sometimes much of the night. We conduct business, make arrangements, or just contact acquaintances to discuss, among other things, how hectic our lives have become. With the line tied up most of the time, who knows what calls never get through?

BE STILL & KNOW THAT I AM GOD

psalm 46:10

*T*he art shows are longer and more frequent. Everyone puts in extra hours. The phone rings incessantly. Time must be found to get presents for the children, the parents, a few friends. The neighbors are having a holiday party. Will I join them after work? It is Advent, but my mood often seems more harried than joyous. There really is no escape from most of this activity. The sense of peace I desire must be found in remembering that the generosity of gift giving, the warmth of fellowship, and the beauty of the lights we put on trees and in windows can all be good, even sanctified, but only when they reflect the love and the light of the Father of lights.

The red letters in the tree spell *Immanuel,* "God with us."

Every good gift And every perfect gift is from above cometh down from the Father of lights

JAMES 1:17

I was at the airport to pick up a friend whose flight had been delayed. Waiting, I became gradually aware of the people around me. The scene was so familiar, almost universal. There was sporadic small talk and the usual sense of tedium combined with hints of anxiety as other flights, too, seemed to be more or less behind schedule. Intermittently, arrivals were announced over the public-address system. Talk halted as eyes expectantly scanned the incoming throng.

Then something wonderful happened. A woman with an infant in her arms caught sight of her husband. He saw her. It might have been safer to walk through a laser beam than through their gaze. A man saw a perhaps long-lost brother. Children were reunited with their parents. In each instance, as they moved toward one another, arms outstretched, I saw the change, the transfiguration, the light on their faces. (Would they need veils like the one Moses wore after meeting the Lord on Mount Sinai?) What I felt was an intimation of the tenderness in the blessing given to Aaron for the children of Israel.

THE·LORD
bless thee and keep thee ⁜

THE·LORD *make his face to shine upon thee, and be gracious unto thee* ⁜

THE·LORD *lift up his countenance*

upon thee and give thee peace ⁜   NUMBERS 6:24-26

have selected from chapters 29 and 30 of Jeremiah words that speak of hope and obedience, words that speak of the Lord's commitment and of His great affection for us.

Our son Joshua recently moved out of the house. He is twenty-one. When days go by and we don't hear from him, I grow anxious. "Don't forget to phone. Please stay in touch," I remind him, reminding myself. We will always be father and son. I will always be glad to help or guide or encourage him. I experience a special joy to have him join us at home for a Sunday dinner.

As we acknowledge and honor this human bond, the greater bond that we both have to our Creator and Redeemer becomes more vital. Its demands become clearer, its promise brighter.

JEREMiah

for I know the plans
that I have for you-
declares the Lord-
plans to prosper you,
not to harm you,
plans to give you hope
and a future..
and when you seek me
with all your heart
you will surely find me..
and you will be my people
and I will be your God.

selections from
chapters twenty-nine and
thirty, niv.

have overheard these words about this picture: "We have that one at our summer cabin in the Blue Ridge Mountains. It expresses so well the sense of peace we feel every time we go there."

I have no question that this psalm speaks of the Lord—not the hills—as the Source of my help. But I also recognize the specific and individual ways the Lord uses all of creation to comfort us, inspire us, instruct us, and delight us.

I will lift up mine eyes unto the hills, from whence cometh my help. My help cometh from the Lord which made heaven and earth.

Psalm 121

cclesiastes comments, "Truly the light is sweet, and a pleasant thing it is for the eyes to behold the sun." The apostle John proclaims, "God is light."

Early one afternoon last spring I was driving home across the James River Bridge. It was the first warm, clear day of the year. The sunlight shimmering on the water not only dazzled me but also made me happy and grateful. The weather had been cold and the days gray and wet for so long that this dancing, brilliant light was suddenly as welcome, and its meaning as unmistakable, as a long-awaited letter from a friend: "Just wanted you to know you are on My mind, Michael. I knew the sunshine would make you glad. Think of it as a reminder of My love."

*D*abar in Hebrew means "word." But it also means the "thing" itself, or "deed." I want the design to express this concept: the "word" becoming the "thing."

By simply speaking the word *light,* God created light. It is part of our heritage and responsibility that to some extent this power has been shared with us. Out of our thoughts come crimes or blessings. Our words darken or lighten a room.

LET THERE BE LIGHT

ight was created when God said, "Let there be light." The "Word" in the gospel of John is much the same. The "Word" is the expression of God's mind and will. The "Word" became human and lived among us— talked to us, shared meals with us, played with our children, taught us, healed us, loved us.

✛ ✛ ✛

Don't you remember? (It wasn't that long ago.) We'd gone down to the beach. It was a warm day. I think a couple of families were having a picnic. We talked about going swimming. Then we noticed a large crowd of people gathered at the water's edge. I said, "Let's see what's going on over there." So we joined them. A small fishing boat bobbed gently on the swells a few yards offshore. A man sat in the boat speaking to the crowd. Even before we began to understand what He was saying—ostensibly a story about a farmer sowing seed—the man Himself seemed extraordinary to us. "Full of grace and truth"—there is no more accurate way to describe Him. As we listened to Him, to the sound of His voice, as we felt the way He looked at us, He had an effect on me that I find impossible to describe. I can say this much. I knew, standing there on the beach that afternoon, that I loved Him.

The blending of color from pale blue to earth red symbolizes the transition from Spirit to flesh.

and
the word
became
flesh
and
dwelt
among
us
full
of grace
and
truth

hapter 24 in the book of Joshua makes the assumption that we are all bound into service of some kind. The challenge is this: Whom, or what, will we serve? Joshua asked the Israelites, "So who will it be? The old Egyptian gods? The Amorite gods?" He didn't add wealth, power, glamour, or pleasure, but I suppose he could have.

I intend the light in one window to represent a home in which this choice, this commitment, is being made.

And once I have made this choice for myself and, insofar as possible, for my household—what then? An immediate conversion to peace and cooperation? Hardly.

Yet I know that in the midst of whatever chaos and strife the human condition may produce, we can as individuals and as a family turn to the Lord, and He will be faithful to help and comfort and guide us.

CHOOSE
THIS DAY
WHOM
YOU WILL
SERVE
BUT AS FOR
ME &
MY HOUSE
WE WILL
SERVE
THE LORD.

*T*he preceding verse from Joshua challenges me to make the choice each day to serve the Lord. Here Deuteronomy confronts me with essentially the same choice: to choose good, to choose life. Today life comes upon me disguised quaintly as a woman speaking over the telephone who thinks I need to subscribe to a television cable service. Life comes upon me as a late snow and daffodils and cardinals at the bird feeder—all somehow sharing the same stage on this March morning outside my studio window. Life comes with the mail that brings news of births as well as illnesses among friends. I also learn of two marriages and a death. Later I have an argument with a man. The words are loud and angry. I feel sick.

In the afternoon my son walks in. "Just thought I'd stop by and see you for a little while, Dad, before I go to work. I haven't eaten. Want to go get a sandwich and coffee?" Beethoven's Violin Concerto is on the car radio. We eat and talk. I begin to feel better.

What a day! Family. Friends. Strangers. A violent climate in the heart and in the air. A chance to destroy. A promise to heal.

The sudden shock, the almost painful beauty of the red feathers against the snow.

That tender, gallant music.

Who could say no to life when it comes bearing such startling gifts as these? Or refuse to participate in a drama that is so appalling and yet so joyful?

Before you this day·
there is set good and
evil·life and death·

C·H·O·O·S·E

LIFE

that both you & your·
descendants·might
live·Excerpts from
Deuteronomy ch.30

We have just gone through a particularly harsh and arduous winter, so Solomon's words sound a special note of reassurance.

From a little clearing in the woods—covered with snow two weeks ago—a light breeze carries the scent of early daffodils to my studio door. The soft cooing of doves awakens the heart from its long, cold silence. The sudden, startling hint of warmth in the air seems to call my name. What beckons is the promise of the Resurrection. It is everywhere.

The beloved bride says, "He brought me to the banqueting house, and his banner over me was love." That banner is over our heads, too, on this gentle spring evening.

Lo, the winter is past, the rains are over and gone and the song of the dove is heard in our land.

eyond the obvious "Why me, Lord?" further relevance of this Scripture can be discerned. It addresses the feeling we sometimes have of wandering about, dislocated, in some modern Sinai Desert, full of doubt and fear.

The path ahead, what we can see of it, looks utterly impossible. We point this out to God. He says, "Don't worry about it." "Don't worry about it?" we say. "There are wild animals out there and terrible hardships and all sorts of dangers." He says, "I know about all that, but it's all right because I will be with you. I will never abandon you or forsake you. I love you."

PHARAOH & BRING THE ISRAELITES OUT OF EGYPT? & GOD SAID WHO AM I, THAT I SHOULD GO TO

I will be with you

BOOK OF EXODUS III·XI·XII

*T*he part about loving God seems reasonable, and maybe, at least in an idealistic way, we do. But then it gets difficult. Love myself? Love my neighbor? After putting aside for a brief, anxious moment ego's contributions to self-esteem, what is there even to like, let alone love? And as for the neighbor . . . well, the promotion of mutual self-interest isn't quite the same thing as love.

So the question is, *How* do you do it? *How* do you love your neighbor as yourself? I don't know. One idea I have is that the matter of choice is crucial.

I was talking about this to one of my sons recently: "Suppose you are in an emotional conflict with me, let's say, or with your girlfriend, or with your brother, or just within yourself. Okay. Now imagine you are in a library. You look at all the titles lining the shelves. You are free to choose whichever one you want. There is *Anger* (one of the several hundred copies the library keeps; it's checked out so frequently). Over there is *Fear*, another best-seller. There is *Guilt*, also, and a subtle little volume called *Indifference*. Fortunately, *Love* is on the shelf, too. If you will choose *that* book, instead of any of the others, the Holy Spirit will honor your choice and will help you read it."

Thou shalt love the Lord thy God ✢ with all thy heart, and with all thy mind, and with all thy soul ✢ This is the first and great commandment ✢ And the second is like unto it : thou shalt love thy neighbor as thyself ✢

THE GOSPEL OF SAINT MATTHEW · CHAPTER 22 : VERSES 37-39

*T*he first line from Isaiah 53:6 represents the Shepherd's staff; the design then becomes a cross as the verse concludes with the Savior's sacrifice.

Most of us are proud to say that we were brought up to be independent and self-reliant. I am. If I need something, I go get it. And this is a good thing, as far as it goes. However, human strength and ability are limited, and at crucial times useless, as when we are confronted with any of the major crises of the spirit: mortality, of course, but also hatred, guilt, fear, pride.

In 2 Corinthians 12:9, we read, "My strength is made perfect in weakness." It's all right to say, "Okay, I guess I need some help here." Help will come, but need must be admitted. It is a fact—simple in theory, difficult in practice—that was made a little easier for me by the following analogy. (I no longer recollect its source.)

Say I find myself in very tight economic circumstances. I'm even ransacking the sofa cushions looking for loose change. I hear a knock on the door. It's an old friend who says, "There is a group of us going out to dinner. Why don't you join us?" "I'd like to," I say, "but I'm broke." "That doesn't matter," my friend answers me, "I have plenty of money. I will pay for you. Please come with us."

I believe this is grace.

All we like sheep have gone astray · we have turned everyone to his own way · and the Lord

✤ hath laid on Him the iniquity of us all.

friend of mine was very sick. The bronchitis he suffered from made sleep at night difficult. By dawn he would be exhausted from sleeplessness and coughing. Somehow, the morning light coming through the bedroom window gave him a sense of ease, and he would drink a little hot tea. I propped pillows behind him, and he would sleep until the midafternoon. He recovered, yet I most vividly associate this psalm with the long ordeal of those nights.

My soul waiteth for the Lord more than they that watch for the morning Psalm 130 ✧ verses 5 & 6 ✧ I wait for the Lord ✧ and in his word do I hope ✧

I was visiting with friends in Maryland. Their neighbors' house had been destroyed in a fire the month before. My friends and many members of their church community had freely undertaken the rebuilding. By the time of my visit the job was nearly completed. As a way of participating—at least in spirit—I sent this design from Psalm 127 as a gift for the new home. I suggested that everyone who worked on the rebuilding might want to sign the back of the picture. The family's return to their new home provided an occasion for a great celebration. My friends told me that everyone present was in wholehearted agreement with the message of the psalm, and that even the young children added their names.

Psalm 127:v.1 ✠ Unless the Lord builds the house ✠ Those who build it labour in vain ✠

*A*friend of mine, a doctor in North Carolina, asked me to illustrate and letter these words from the gospel of Matthew. He has an extensive geriatric practice, and he wanted this Scripture to remind him that beyond the physical frailty—beyond the occasional fears, depressions, and mental vagueness—he was encountering in each patient another and a much deeper reality. It is the reality of Jesus Christ who, in another part of the Gospels, tells us, "A new commandment I give unto you, that ye love one another as I have loved you . . ."

Inasmuch as ye have done it unto one of the least

of these my brethren, ye have done it unto me.

riginally I designed this piece as a gift for a friend. For weeks he had been trying to get me to join the church choir. I wasn't sure I had the time, I told him, and besides I had no musical aptitude. He said they practiced once a week, he'd pick me up, and not to worry about the music, he'd help me.

I eventually did join the choir. I don't think I ever sang particularly well, but I did enjoy it. We sang this part of Psalm 51 as the offertory every Sunday.

In addition to being a uniquely appropriate gift for my friend, this psalm has another personal meaning. Many years ago a minister and his wife, my hosts during a trip to Georgia, told me about "breath prayers." "Find a prayer," they said, "a prayer you love, but it must be short. The first half of the prayer you speak, or think, as you draw in a breath; the second half, as you let the breath out. It should be a prayer of supplication." Ever since then, random moments of my days and nights have been filled with (*breathe in*), "Create in me a clean heart, O God," (*breathe out*) "and renew a right spirit within me."

1. Have mercy upon me, O God, according to thy lovingkindness: according to the multitude of thy tender mercies blot out my transgressions 10. Create in me a clean heart, O God, & renew a right spirit within me. 11. Cast me not away from thy presence; and take not thy holy spirit from me. 12. Restore unto me the joy of thy salvation; and uphold me with thy free spirit. Verses 1, 10, 11, and 12 from the 51st psalm.

*P*eter asked Jesus, "When my brother wrongs me, how often should I forgive him? Seven times?" "Not seven times," Jesus answered, "but seventy times seven." The theme of forgiveness is further symbolized by the crosslike representation of the number four.

There is a small dark cell in which a heart has been imprisoned for years. Jesus' teaching on forgiveness aims to unlock that cell. The answer to seventy times seven is freedom.

Forgiveness

*T*he strength and dignity in the Roman alphabet strike me as just right for proclaiming the names of God.

"And the government shall be upon his shoulder." These are the words in Isaiah that precede the titles of praise. "Of the increase of his government and peace there shall be no end" are the words that follow.

So where is this government? And when will this "mighty God" actually come to power?

The apostles must have been brooding over questions like these—with their obvious political implications—when they asked Jesus if He planned to restore the kingdom to Israel.

The answer they got, and the one we still get, is simply that God is in control, that the Holy Spirit will enable us to be witnesses for Christ, and that the government He has in mind is not located in a parliament or a palace or any other seat of temporal authority. The permanent location this mighty God envisions for His government is the conscience of a human being. The liberation He brings is of the heart.

*T*he dove and heart design is meant as a symbol of peace entering our lives. Later in the gospel of John, Jesus is very definite about the fact that this peace is of the Spirit and not of the world. In the world, He says, we will be rejected, wronged, persecuted. Indeed, He anticipates this.

Throughout every tribulation, however, we are encouraged to be joyful, to remember that the world after all is not our home, that we are visitors here, stewards, servants to our God who tells us—in Isaiah 43:1—"Fear not: for I have redeemed thee, I have called thee by thy name; thou art mine."

MY
PEACE
I GIVE UNTO
YOU

THEREFORE
LET NOT
YOUR
HEART
BE TROUBLED
NEITHER
LET IT
BE
AFRAID
·
Saint John
14/27

*A*s we read on through Proverbs, the opposing imagery is just as prominent and all too familiar: "a heavy heart," "a broken spirit drieth the bones."

A merry heart? How is it possible? It is a gift, but perhaps it begins by wanting it, by anticipating it. Just as we remain in contact—often across time and great distance—with family and friends, I think we can faithfully expect "letters from home." They contain messages of encouragement, humor, beauty. They are often subtle, but they do arrive, punctually, like the sunrise, if we look for them.

When I picked some early sweet peas last April and brought them into my studio, a friend commented, "They have this particular scent, you see, because God knew it would please us."

A merry
heart
doeth good
like
a medicine

PROVERBS 17:22

have owned sheep, and because of my memory of their defenselessness, their reliance on the shepherd, this symbol for our relationship with God seems to me ideal.

As for the psalm itself, it is so familiar, I confess, I don't always focus on the individual words. Sometimes the sounds of the well-known phrases—"The Lord is my shepherd," "He restoreth my soul," "I will fear no evil"—become a kind of music, like that a lamb might have heard from the shepherd's lyre while resting in green pastures. Perhaps they are like the music to which the psalms were first sung, a music that takes away fear, a music of comfort and loving-kindness. The sound of this psalm being spoken is the music of our faith.

The blue of "still waters," the green of pastures, the gold of oil, are some of the color references.

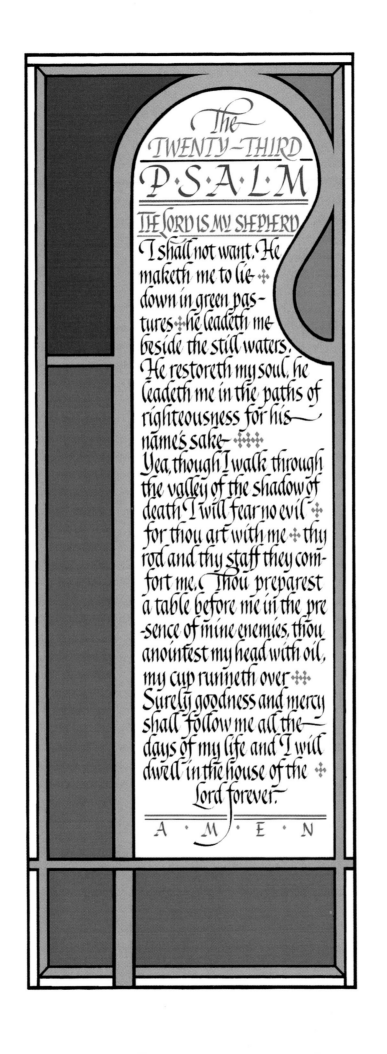

The
TWENTY–THIRD
P·S·A·L·M
THE LORD IS MY SHEPHERD
I shall not want. He
maketh me to lie
down in green pas-
tures, he leadeth me
beside the still waters.
He restoreth my soul, he
leadeth me in the paths of
righteousness for his
name's sake.
Yea, though I walk through
the valley of the shadow of
death, I will fear no evil,
for thou art with me, thy
rod and thy staff they comfort me. Thou preparest
a table before me in the pre
-sence of mine enemies, thou
anointest my head with oil,
my cup runneth over.
Surely goodness and mercy
shall follow me all the
days of my life and I will
dwell in the house of the
Lord forever.
A · M · E · N

*T*t was an early spring morning, almost dawn. I was driving across rural North Carolina on my way home from an art show. Through the stillness and mist, I caught glimpses of cattle standing motionless in a field, a tractor at the end of a furrow, a window in which a light had just been turned on, others still dark. (God perhaps gently saying, "Oh, I'll let them sleep just a little longer.") At some point, while I had been driving through the night, He had evidently decided to do it again, to create another day, and there I was to see it from the beginning and to "rejoice and be glad in it."

The black letters represent the horizon, the curve of red script the rising sun of a new day.

THIS IS THE DAY

THIS·IS·THE·DAY·WHICH·THE·LORD·HATH·MADE...

Let us rejoice and be glad in it.

psalms 118:24

*S*ome of the connections I have made between a particular Scripture and my own experience involve driving. The fact is, I exhibit widely and spend a good deal of time on the road. If I am making my way through the mountains to, say, West Virginia, and the road is unfamiliar, and the fog lies dense, and I see a yellow sign that says, "Sharp curve ahead. Slow to 20 mph," I will not think of this as interference or as a restriction of my freedom. I will quite rightly, and gratefully, realize that someone is trying to help me save my life.

The 10 Commandments

1. Thou shalt have no other gods before me.

2. Thou shalt not make unto thee any graven image.

3. Thou shalt not take the name of the Lord thy God in vain.

4. Remember the Sabbath day, to keep it holy.

6. Thou shalt not kill.

5. Honor thy father and thy mother.

7. Thou shalt not commit adultery.

8. Thou shalt not steal.

10. Thou shalt not covet.

9. Thou shalt not bear false witness against thy neighbor.

The twentieth chapter from the Book of Exodus verses three to seventeen

*T*his is an adaptation of Galatians 5:22–23. The first phrase, the reference to the Spirit, is shown as the branch or vine. The fruits, or gifts—peace, love, joy, and the rest—grow out of it.

The loose, flowing design of the letters suggests freedom, since that is the effect of the Spirit in our lives. Yet in the distribution of weight and color, and in the interconnections of the words, there is also discipline.

It is also the balance of freedom and discipline that Paul is talking about earlier in Galatians when he says that we have been made free, not to do wrong, but to love and serve one another.

Gentleness · Faithfulness · Patience · Joy · Love · The Fruits of the Spirit · Self Control · Peace · Goodness and Kindness · Galatians 5: 22 23

*J*ust as Paul speaks to us about the seeming contradiction of freedom and obedience in Galatians, he is telling us here that our true individuality exists only in the context of harmonious interaction within a greater collective body. He tells us that the members of that body are meant to complement one another, like hand-eye coordination on the physical level, and that fulfillment does not come with strife and rivalry or with isolation.

In this illustration the starry multitude is meant to represent the multitude of souls whose combined individualities make up the body of Christ. We need one another.

In my experience, only because members of my family and a few stalwart friends are willing to help me is it possible to share these designs and Scriptures as I do. A picture from our gallery can arrive on someone's doorstep in Columbus, Ohio, because, in addition to the initial creative impulse, there have been many unique individual contributions of skill, diligence, patience, humor, intelligence, and faith.

My hope is that as these ideas are read and reread over the years, they will be translated into action. My hope is that they will, in combination with the work and the ideas of others, become a part of that greater body, the body of Christ.

FOR·AS
THE BODY

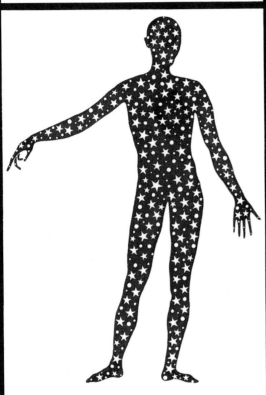

IS·ONE

and hath many members ✦ and all these members are one body ✦ so also is Christ. For by one Spirit are we ✦ all baptized into one body,

whether we be Jews or Gentiles, whether we be bond or free. For the body is not one member, but many ✦ If the foot shall say "Because I am not the hand, I am not of the body," is it therefore not of the body? And if ✦ the ear shall say "Because I am not the eye, I am not of the body," is it therefore not of the body? The eye cannot say unto the hand "I have no need of thee." If one member suffers, all members suffer with it, and if one be honoured, all rejoice with it ✦ God hath put all these separate members into the body with a purpose. It is the body of Christ Ye are that body ✦

Excerpts from St. Paul's first letter to the Corinthians, chapter 12, verses 12 through 27 ✦

*P*aul sits in prison while he writes these words. (Indeed, the main body of the text is enclosed in a tight rectangle.) His mind and his spirit, however, are free. And through this cheerful letter to his friends in Philippi, he is communicating to me, across the years, that I, too, can live outside the confines and tribulations of any material situation. Paul tells me that feelings of freedom and joy are as direct a result of the thoughts I think as feelings of physical well-being are of the food I eat.

Paul promises that as our thoughts become focused on what is true, noble, and lovely, our lives will become a reflection of these qualities, and that in this way we will find peace.

Whatsoever things are:

TRUE
NOBLE
RIGHT AND
PURE ✦
LOVELY
ADMIRABLE
EXCELLENT
AND
PRAISE
-WORTHY ✦

think on
these things.

phil. 4:8

A frequent response: "I like the lilies. It's just never been clear to me what that Scripture means."

What it means to me—briefly—is, "Quit worrying." And, no, I don't think Jesus is recommending idleness. The Bible contains too much encouragement to diligence, in Proverbs, for example, for me to assume that industry would be discouraged in the Gospels. I think we are meant to be not only responsible and creative, but also dependent, trusting, and reliant. Perhaps the issue lies in our priorities. Later, in the same chapter of Matthew, Jesus speaks of the Father's great generosity, "Seek ye first the kingdom of God, and his righteousness; and all these things shall be added unto you."

CONSIDER THE LILIES

OF THE FIELD

how they grow; they toil not,
neither do they spin, and yet I
say unto you that even Solomon
in all his glory was not arrayed
like one of these. Matthew 6:28

We see Job in the dark pit of his anguish and affliction. Yet even there—as the stars of light descending from heaven illustrate—he is not isolated from God.

In my understanding of this strange drama, a few problems remain stubbornly unresolved. Nevertheless, I find in it great treasures. The grandeur of God's voice comes out of the whirlwind. And He challenges Job with all these curious and extraordinary questions: "Where is the dwelling of light and darkness? Who will feed the raven and his children? Who puts wisdom in the mind and numbers the clouds?" And of course, finally, triumphantly—"I know that my Redeemer liveth"—Job's steadfast certainty of his relationship with God anchors him amid inexplicable suffering.

Though he slay me yet will i trust in Him

job

*I*n reading the Bible I often try to visualize the physical setting. I imagine the weather, the looks in people's eyes, the sounds of their voices, the unrecorded reactions such as the neighbor who, after the Sermon on the Mount, might clap Jesus on the shoulder and say, "That was a real good talk You gave there, son. The thing I want to know is, You think You're ever going to get that cabinet shop of Yours off the ground?" I imagine the miracles and mighty works Jesus did, things John tells us are not even written. I wonder what mighty works Jesus will do, mighty works that Paul says are far beyond all we can ask or imagine.

Of course, these various images and speculations are not represented as the truth per se, but as a device that, for me, makes particular Scriptures living and vivid.

✝ ✝ ✝

Jesus pauses a long moment after the words "the kingdom of God is within you." The Pharisees, thinking He has finished, have begun to leave. Then in a voice so soft and reflective that only those standing closest to Him even hear, He adds casually, almost as an afterthought, "Oh, by the way, hell is, too." Those who hear this are startled, of course. They turn and take a step back toward Him. "What did You say?" He looks at them thoughtfully, considers, and then says, "Ah . . . never mind. I'll tell you another time."

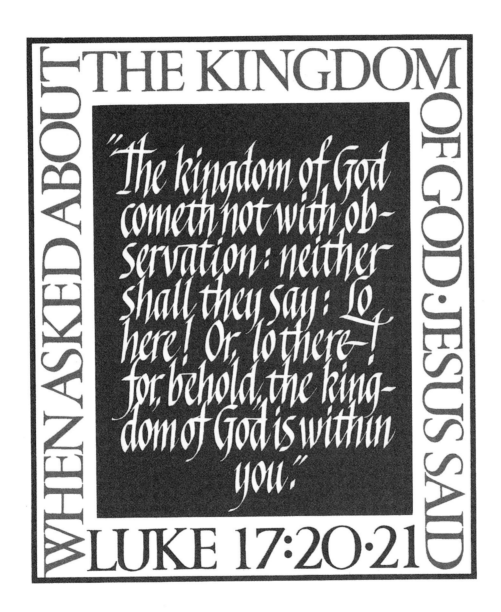

WHEN ASKED ABOUT THE KINGDOM OF GOD JESUS SAID

"The kingdom of God cometh not with observation: neither shall they say: Lo here! Or, lo there! for behold, the kingdom of God is within you."

LUKE 17:20·21

*T*he placement of the text within the letter *U*—the way it is contained and enclosed—is meant as a symbol of security. Paradoxically it is security we find in surrender.

TRUST

in the Lord with all thine
heart ✦ and lean not unto
thine own understanding,
in all thy ways acknow ✦
ledge him and he shall
✦ direct thy paths, Pr.
chapter 3, ver. 5&6

We have all experienced the crisis of guests dropping in unannounced.

Many years ago I lived on a farm in a remote section of northern California. At a little after 3:00 one morning in midsummer I awoke to the loud snapping of apple boughs in our densely overgrown driveway, the roar of a diesel engine, and headlights outside my bedroom window. The commotion, I soon discovered, was caused by the arrival of a band of singers and musicians in a large bus, stopping by on their way to San Francisco. There were the performers and their helpers and their families and their dogs. A friend of mine, a frequent houseguest, knew the manager of the band and had once casually suggested he drop in sometime. He had no recollection of inviting the whole troupe.

It was a warm night, so after great quantities of tea and toast and jam had been consumed (with impromptu meals for thirty-five, the menu is limited), I guided my guests to a spacious barn where a few days earlier we had—providentially—put in a truckload of fresh hay. Then I went back to bed and slept until about 8:00 when I was again awakened by an unfamiliar sound. It was music this time. I looked out the window and there, wandering through the unmowed grass of the orchard, was a young man. Blond, tanned, barefoot, shirtless, he was playing a trumpet. Notes in long, graceful, golden ribbons floated through the bright morning air. The sunlight glinted off the trumpet and off the drops of dew that still hung from the apple boughs.

Musicians praise God with their music: I praise Him for their music.

I lay down again and thought, *If I could hear sunlight, this is how it would sound.*

Something I at first see as a problem or a burden often turns out like that. Beneath a disturbing or unattractive wrapping, I am surprised by a gift of singular beauty, a moment of joy, a hint of glory.

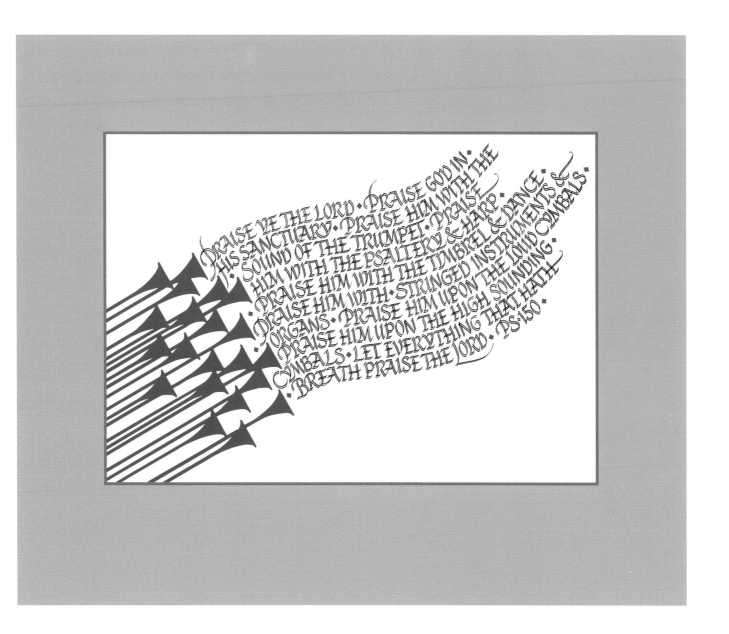

My intention was to create a representation of death: the severed tree trunk followed by a reaffirmation of life—the brave, tiny, new green leaf. The light of the new day could be Easter morning.

Martin Luther said that the story of the Resurrection is written not only in the Gospels, but on every leaf in the forest and on every flower in the field each spring.

Behold, I make all things new!

have felt the violence and the horror of death hit me and friends and family with such force that nothing remained but the broken remnants of our lives and the varieties of pain. Like a crystal glass that had fallen from a great height, all life seemed to lie in fragments.

At that point, when human resources could scarcely do more than assess the wreckage, a quiet voice said, "Give Me the broken pieces. I'm really quite good at this. Restoration is one of My specialties. When I'm finished, that glass will be as good as new. In fact, it will be better than new."

✦ ✦ ✦

The odd, bouncing movement of the layout and letter design of this verse from the twenty-first chapter of Revelation is meant to suggest and anticipate celebration, even exuberance.

enesis 1 says, "Let there be a firmament in the midst of the waters." An image of heavens and seas, earth and sun and moon springs forth. The gospel of John signals the central position of Jesus Christ in creation: "In the beginning was the Word." The text is based on Psalms 148 and 150. These verses remind me of Beethoven's "Ode to Joy." All the members of creation—men and women; babies and angels; stars and planets; clouds, rain, fire, and snow; mountains, hills, and forests; fish and birds and beasts of the field—are gathered up into a vast, irresistible chorus of exultation and praise.

If you are interested in purchasing other Michael Podesta products, please visit your local bookstore, or contact Michael directly at the phone number or address below:

1-800-922-3595

Michael Podesta
8847 Eclipse Drive
Suffolk, VA 23433